mahikan ka onot
The Poetry of Duncan Mercredi

mahikan ka onot
The Poetry of Duncan Mercredi

Selected
with an
introduction by
Warren Cariou
and an
afterword by
Duncan Mercredi

Wilfrid Laurier University Press acknowledges the support of the Canada Council for the Arts for our publishing program. We acknowledge the financial support of the Government of Canada through the Canada Book Fund for our publishing activities. This work was supported by the Research Support Fund.

 Canada Council for the Arts / Conseil des arts du Canada

Library and Archives Canada Cataloguing in Publication

Title: Mahikan ka onot : the poetry of Duncan Mercredi / selected with an introduction by Warren Cariou and an afterword by Duncan Mercredi.
Other titles: Poems. Selections | Poetry of Duncan Mercredi
Names: Mercredi, Duncan, 1951– author, writer of afterword. | Cariou, Warren, 1966– editor, writer of introduction.
Series: Laurier poetry series.
Description: Series statement: Laurier poetry series | Includes bibliographical references.
Identifiers: Canadiana (print) 2020029654X | Canadiana (ebook) 20200297422 |
    ISBN 9781771124744 (softcover) | ISBN 9781771124751 (EPUB) |
    ISBN 9781771124768 (PDF)
Classification: LCC PS8576.E722 A6 2020 | DDC C811/.54—dc23

Front cover image: *We are the Moon* by David Hallet. Cover design by Gary Blakeley. Interior design by Mike Bechthold.

© 2020 Wilfrid Laurier University Press
Waterloo, Ontario, Canada
www.wlupress.wlu.ca

This book is printed on FSC® certified paper. It contains recycled materials and other controlled sources, is processed chlorine free, and is manufactured using biogas energy.

Printed in Canada

Every reasonable effort has been made to acquire permission for copyright material used in this text, and to acknowledge all such indebtedness accurately. Any errors and omissions called to the publisher's attention will be corrected in future printings.

No part of this publication may be reproduced, stored in a retrieval system, or transmitted, in any form or by any means, without the prior written consent of the publisher or a licence from the Canadian Copyright Licensing Agency (Access Copyright). For an Access Copyright licence, visit http://www.accesscopyright.ca or call toll free to 1-800-893-5777.

Dedicated to my family and to the people of Misipawistik, annoying as I can be, they gave me a voice and a medium to share that voice.
—Duncan Mercredi

Table of Contents

Foreword, *Brian Henderson and Neil Besner* / ix
A Little Bit About Me (Biographical Note) / xi
Introduction, *Warren Cariou* / xiii

from *Spirit of the Wolf: Raise Your Voice* (1991)
    Spirit of the Wolf / 1
    A Remembering Smile / 2
    Broken Glass / 4
    scraps of paper / 5
    mask / 6
    as the walls came up / 7
    the final solution / 8
    Mothers / 9
    Gabriel (Buffalo Hunt) / 10
    mahikan (Wolf) / 12
    Forgotten Words / 13
    Betty / 14
    A Gathering / 16

from *Dreams of the Wolf in the City* (1992)
    Black Robe / 17
    dreams of the wolf in the city / 18
    crazy face junior gone wild / 20
    Lake Winnipeg 1956 / 22
    highway 75 1991 / 22
    Lake Winnipeg 1956 (2) / 23
    highway 75 1991 (2) / 23
    Lake Winnipeg 1956 highway 75 1991 / 24
    the sun rises red / 25
    three in the morning / 27

fort and york / 28
something you said / 30
strangers / 31
Sandilands / 33

from *Wolf and Shadows* (1995)
wolf and shadows / 35
traditional smoke / 36
blue collar blues / 37
statue / 38
spring / 40
tripping back / 41
eagle woman sky flyer (revised) / 42
where dreams begin / 44

from *Duke of Windsor: Wolf Sings the Blues* (1997)
street poetry / 45
nine streets past crazy / 47
snowbound / 49
howl / 50
we are wolf / 51
vision quest / 52
on this day / 53
yesterday's song / 54

New and Uncollected Poems (1997–2019)
this city is red / 55
Three solitudes / 58
Getting jiggie / 61
omasinayikesis / 62
Drowning / 63
Tin can skates / 64
who will wipe my tears / 66
iskotawan / 67

Afterword, *Duncan Mercredi* / 69
Acknowledgements / 77

Foreword

The Laurier Poetry Series was conceived in 2002 as a means to celebrate Canadian poetry and to introduce new readers to the richness and diversity of its poets. Rather than curate another large anthology that featured only a few poems by each poet, we thought it a better idea to suggest the real range of a poet's work by enlarging the selection. Our anthology would have to comprise many volumes. But why persist with a traditional anthology? Why not create a series of small and affordable volumes, each devoted to the work of a single poet? Each volume could be introduced by a knowledgeable reader, familiar with the poet's work and addressing it in greater depth than in normal anthologies; and each volume could close with the poet contributing an afterword such as no standard anthology could offer.

Readers could pick and choose which poets they wanted to explore; instructors could also pick and choose combinations of volumes in a package for their students—and could change this selection from semester to semester. And the volumes could reach an international audience. Each would also have the potential to open out onto other books by the featured poet.

That was the blueprint. The Series was launched in 2004, with Catherine Hunter's selection of the poetry of Lorna Crozier, *Before the First Word*. There have been over thirty volumes since, offering introductions to a wide range of poets and poetries, and more are in the works. The Laurier Poetry Series is now the most comprehensive collection of Canadian poetries in print anywhere. All volumes are also available as digital editions.

We are continuously grateful for the consummate professionalism of the team at Wilfrid Laurier University Press which has ensured that these sometimes technically tricky volumes are presented accurately and beautifully. In particular, we would like to acknowledge the invaluable work of Managing Editor Rob Kohlmeier, who oversaw production of the Series from its beginning until his retirement in 2020.

At this time we would also like to welcome Tanis MacDonald to the editorial team. Tanis is a professor of creative writing and English at WLU and a fine poet in her own right.

What continues to inspire us about the LPS is its reception across the country. The love and art and passion and intimacy that thirty-plus editors and thirty-plus poets have brought to their volumes; the innumerable hours and conversations and meetings; the thousands of emails between and among poets and editors and the staff at WLU Press; the generous reviews in the country's journals; the reception in classrooms and beyond: all of this eloquently speaks to the joyful proliferation of poetry in Canada today.

With each new volume, LPS hopes to continue to recognize the growing provenance of this wealth, the wide range of these riches. Our poets—and their readers—deserve nothing less.

—*Brian Henderson and Neil Besner*
General Editors

x / *Foreword*

A Little Bit About Me (Biographical Note)

A little bit about me, born in Misipawistik (Grand Rapids) Manitoba. I grew up in that small northern village and lived in a two storey log cabin with my kookum (grandmother), father and mother. The early years surrounded by an older brother, older sister, younger brother and younger sister and probably about 20 cousins, all within walking distance. I helped my father with his dogs, fishing and some trapping. I wasn't much of a hunter, so my father gave up on trying to make me one but my kookum told him to leave me alone, my path was taking me on another journey.

I left Misipawistik when I was 16 to attend high school in Cranberry Portage, MB. I worked for the Department of Highways maintenance division during summer breaks from school. After graduation I worked for the Department of Highways Construction Surveys. The two years with the department, went from Misipawistik to Minago River, William Lake bush camps located next to Highway No. 6. When that job was completed I was sent to Soab Lake, a little lake situated between Waboden and Thompson, MB. My next stop would have been a camp between Thompson and Nelson House but decided against it. I hadn't spent much time with my daughter who was born during my time at Minago River, it was time to go home.

I worked for a summer with a carpenter contractor but it was not a full time position and with two daughters I had no option but seek a steady job.

Later that summer I landed work with Manitoba Hydro and was sent to 8 Mile Channel, a bush camp located near Playgreen Lake and Lake Winnipeg, about a two hour drive from Norway House. When summer came I went back to Winnipeg, my partner was expecting and I decided against going back up north.

I found a job with the Department of Highways, Land Surveys Division, it meant being away from home but only five days a week and home on the weekends. Twenty three years later, Indian and Northern Affairs Canada (INAC) came calling to train their lands unit employees all about land surveys. It was to be for a two year stint which ended up being the strangest twenty two year career.

The month before I retired I decided to put down on paper every place I either stayed in or visited while with the highways department and INAC, I stopped counting after reaching 140. The one thing that has remained with me all those times with the highways and INAC, nearly every motel, hotel I stayed in had the same lime green walls and same carpet design.

Duncan

Works by Duncan Mercredi

Spirit of the Wolf: Raise Your Voice. Winnipeg: Pemmican Publications, 1991.

Dreams of the Wolf in the City. Winnipeg: Pemmican Publications, 1992.

Wolf and Shadows. Winnipeg: Pemmican Publications, 1995.

Duke of Windsor: Wolf Sings the Blues. Winnipeg: Pemmican Publications, 1997.

Introduction

Duncan Mercredi has often resisted being placed in the spotlight, preferring instead to turn everyone's attention toward the brilliant emerging Indigenous writers who have been arriving on the scene for more than a generation now—many of whom he has mentored and supported. But as we have worked together on this book, I've had the opportunity to visit with Duncan more often, and to gain a deeper understanding of his life, his art, and his connections to the land and the people of his home. He has given me permission to share some of the things I've learned in our conversations, so that you can have a better context for the work contained in these pages. Because his poetry is so closely woven into his experiences and his relationships, I feel it is important for readers to be welcomed into the sphere of those relations too. Perhaps the best way to do this is to imagine that you and I are walking together along a trapline, or a dark city street, or a wind-blown highway, and that I'm telling you about someone we are about to meet just around the next corner. His reputation precedes him, but there is so much more to learn.

Upon meeting Duncan, one of the first things you will probably notice is his generous and self-effacing approach to the artist's life. This attitude reminds me of the Cree concept of *peweyimowin*: humility. Putting others forward, being generous when no one is watching, diminishing the importance of your own achievements—these are all aspects of *peweyimowin* as it is lived not only among Cree-speaking peoples, but also in many other Indigenous cultures of Turtle Island. It hardly needs to be said that the practice of *peweyimowin* is highly unusual in the contemporary literary world, and it may not always mesh well with the business side of being a writer, but it is simply a part of who Duncan Mercredi is, and he wouldn't have it any other way. Duncan is allergic to pretension and pomposity, and he has no interest in the machinery of self-promotion, preferring instead to invest all of his creative energy into the work itself, and into fostering the next generation of story-makers.

This approach inevitably shapes his poems themselves. One might say that Duncan Mercredi's poetics are based upon a disdain for bullshit in all of its forms, and a dedication to the truth-telling potential of language. He does not seek acclaim, and yet the directness and energy of his work has made him a figure of great respect in literary and storytelling circles. Duncan's reputation as a writer and storyteller has grown the old-fashioned way, through word of mouth spread by all those who have been captivated by his stories, his poems, and his performances. People recognize that he has lived what he writes about, and that he continues to live it. This is not to say that Duncan's stories and poems are all documentary in nature, but that they come from a place of deep and thoughtful observation. He is well-versed in Cree and Métis storytelling traditions, and he also knows intimately the lived experience of Indigenous people in his homeland, ranging from the city to the highway to the bush. His stories and poems reflect the truths of that experience.

This valuing of truth-telling may well be connected to Duncan's earliest training as a storyteller during his childhood in his home community of Misipawistik (later known as Grand Rapids, Manitoba). Born into a family of Cree and Métis heritage, Duncan was chosen at a young age by his kookum to be the family's story-carrier, and this role involved a great deal of careful study and memory-work, all of which was conducted in his first language, Cree. Duncan often talks about the *ka-pa-gu-ka-chick*, or visitors, the storytellers who came to Misipawistik each winter carrying news of the people's neighbours and relatives along the river. His kookum explained to him the crucial importance of remembering the stories of the *ka-pa-gu-ka-chick* and retelling them accurately: if there were gaps or errors in the retold story, it could distort the community's history or damage someone's reputation. Duncan describes the ways his kookum would test him to be sure he remembered each story, detail by detail. Mistakes would earn him extra household chores, including the most dreaded one: emptying the chamberpot. His kookum applied this teaching technique not only with the stories of the *ka-pa-gu-ka-chick*, but also with the traditional Métis stories she told, many of which involved the Roogaroo, a shapeshifting being that can change between human and wolf form. The Roogaroo would later come to be an important character in Duncan's own performances as well as his poems.

Duncan Mercredi is renowned today for his tellings of those traditional Métis stories he learned from his kookum. He performs many times each year in schools, universities, and storytelling festivals, and he is especially well-known for the interactivity of his performances. There is no fourth wall in a Duncan Mercredi storytelling; audience members become participants in the story, and in a sense they also become community members, if only for the brief time of the performance. As he is telling a story, Duncan transforms himself bodily into the characters, mimicking someone's gait, shifting the register of his voice, creeping or dashing around the room, whispering into an audience member's ear. He shows us how the storyteller can be a kind of shape-changer too.

While many Indigenous poets are also storytellers in an informal way, and virtually all of them are devotees of Indigenous oral traditions, I know of no one other than Duncan Mercredi who is equally skilled as a storyteller and a poet. His balancing of these two practices is unique, and it is clear that his skills in both realms are mutually supportive. His stories are marked by the vivid imagery of a poet, and by a finely honed sensitivity to cadence and wordplay. His public readings of his written work are dazzling performances that go far beyond what is normally suggested by the staid term "poetry reading." Some of his poems, like the audience favourite "this city is red," have continued to change and evolve over many years of performance, like oral stories tend to do. Writing down the poem is sometimes a secondary activity for Duncan in comparison to the performance, which remains the forge of his creativity.

Many of the poems in this collection are also concerned with witnessing Indigenous history and documenting the injustices of colonialism. Like the stories of the *ka-pa-gu-ka-chick*, these poems are directed toward telling and preserving the community's own truths, outside of the distorting mechanisms of colonial history. Some poems, such as "Gabriel (Buffalo Hunt)," gesture back several generations to celebrate the traditional ways of life on the land. Others examine Indigenous experiences of colonial violence in many forms, especially when these histories are largely unacknowledged by settler-colonial culture. Nearly a quarter of a century before the publication of the Truth and Reconciliation Commission's final report, Duncan's poems "Black Robe" and "Forgotten Words" powerfully represented Indigenous people's experiences of abuse, language loss, and cultural disorientation caused by Canada's residential schools program. Ten years before the province of Manitoba issued an official apology for the failure of the justice system in the case of Helen Betty Osborne's brutal murder, Mercredi's poem "Betty" issued a haunting condemnation of the conspiracies of silence that have for so long preserved the fictions of Canada's innocence and benevolence.

Introduction / xv

One crucial event in Misipawistik's history has had a particularly large impact on Duncan Mercredi's life as well as his poems and stories: the construction of the Grand Rapids Dam. Begun in 1960 when Duncan was nine years old and completed in 1968, this Manitoba Hydro megaproject drastically changed life for the people of Misipawistik.[1] The land itself was massively altered, with the flooding of vast areas of hunting and trapping territory, sacred sites, homes, and hunting camps. Even the river was diverted, and the rapids that gave Misipawistik its name were silenced forever. The influx of thousands of construction workers from the south also dramatically affected the community, bringing racism, social inequity, alcohol, and violence, including widespread predation upon the community's women and girls. The traditional hunting and fishing economy was devastated. English became the majority language, and a hierarchical class system began to create divisions in the community. Soon after the river's flow was interrupted, the *ka-pa-gu-ka-chick* no longer brought their stories to Misipawistik.

While there is no single representative "Hydro poem" in *mahikan ka onot*, the impact of Hydro is pervasive throughout the collection. In his storytelling practice, Duncan divides the history of Misipawistik into two different eras: Before Hydro and After Hydro. He also sees the same division in his own life—his traditional Cree/Métis childhood interrupted by the juggernaut of colonial modernity. Soon after the dam became operational, Duncan left Misipawistik, first to work in bush camps and eventually to make a home in Winnipeg. While he has now developed an intimate connection to what he calls his "urban trapline" on the streets of Winnipeg, still he does not forget his early life in Misipawistik and the changes he has lived through. In many of his poems, there is a before and an after, gesturing toward the two phases of Mercredi's life that are bisected by the construction of the dam. In "A Remembering Smile," the narrator walks city streets that are "full of strangers with eyes distant / unseeing," but as he navigates this hostile environment, he takes solace in memories of his childhood, when he lived close to friends and family and he played on a familiar and living landscape, "still hearing the river / the river wild and free / alive." The poem is punctuated by the different sounds the river made throughout the seasons of the narrator's childhood, and it becomes clear that the river itself was a living companion, perhaps even a storyteller, for the people of the community. It is devastating to read this poem with the knowledge that the Saskatchewan River at Misipawistik no longer makes any of those sounds—that the rapids themselves are gone.

Nonetheless, for the narrator, his memory remains a conduit of connection to the land, even when the voice of the river has been silenced by the construction of the dam.

The city is often the landscape of "after" in these poems: after the dam, after displacement, after the residential schools, after environmental damage, after every other symptom of colonization's arrival and entrenchment. Nonetheless, the city is also a place of dreams, of camaraderie, and of burgeoning solidarity, as Indigenous people connect there and form a new kind of community. Duncan Mercredi's work provides a rare look at the history of urban Indigenous people's struggles for empowerment, and their continued efforts to maintain their relationships to the land. Today, more than half of Indigenous people in Canada live in urban centres[2], yet the experience of urban Indigenous people remains underrepresented in literature, film, and music. Duncan's poems resonate with the emotions and the politics behind this statistic. His portrayal of the city is sometimes wary—alert to the omnipresent possibility of discrimination and violence—but also equally open to the energy of Indigenous resistance and resurgence that coalesces on the streets, in coffee shops, in bars. This energy is often expressed in dancing, which is portrayed in these poems as a claim of relationship to the land and to community—a decolonial performance of urban belonging. In "this city is red," his great anthem of Indigenous Winnipeg, he writes "we laugh, we cry, we heal, we dance, we sing, our heartbeat is the drum." While the city is definitely the place of "after" in these poems, this "after" is emphatically not a time of cultural erasure, but a time when resistance and resurgence become the most important modes of Indigenous life.

One question that remains is: who or what are the howling wolves (*mahikanuk ka onot*) of this book? There is not a simple answer to this question, but there are several possibilities. Certainly, the wolf as a character is crucial to Duncan Mercredi's work, as the titles of all his books indicate. In his first book, *Spirit of the Wolf: Raise Your Voice*, the wolf's howl is a kind of call to community, a prompt for other Indigenous voices to join in, to stand up for themselves and to be a part of the group. Anyone who has heard wolves howl will know that this is exactly what they do: one starts the song, and then the others join in. This is particularly meaningful given that the book came into being in the summer of 1990, during the Oka crisis, when the Mohawk community of Kanesetake was under threat from the Canadian army, and a groundswell of support from Indigenous communities across the country forever changed the relationship between Indigenous peoples and the Canadian state. As I have argued in *The Oxford Handbook of Indigenous American Literature*, 1990 is probably the most important year in Canadian Indigenous literary history, because the Oka crisis and its aftermath sparked a flourishing of creativity among Indigenous writers that continues to this day.

Duncan Mercredi came of age as a writer during that tumultuous summer, and in many ways his first book is a direct response to that galvanizing moment, a voice raised in solidarity with his relatives from across Turtle Island. He recalls being part of an extraordinary Indigenous writers' workshop organized by Pemmican Publishers and held in Winnipeg that summer, led by Maria Campbell, Jeannette Armstrong, Lee Maracle, Jordan Wheeler, and several other luminaries of Indigenous literature. The workshop concluded with a public reading at Winnipeg's West End Cultural Centre, where more than 200 audience members witnessed the beginning of a new era in Indigenous literature. It was Duncan Mercredi's first performance as a poet. He signed the contract for his first book with Pemmican Publishers shortly afterward, and he published three more books with them in the following decade.

Another version of the wolf in these poems is the lone wolf, a figure that is reminiscent of many of the narrators—a solitary character who mostly shuns society, but who also observes it from a careful distance. This is especially true of the poems set in the urban space and in the world of labour, where racist reactions to the narrators' Indigeneity often seem to create an uncrossable barrier. The work poems here arise out of Mercredi's many years labouring in the largely non-Indigenous contexts of bush camps and highway survey crews. Some of these pieces reference blue-collar solidarity that crosses the boundaries of settler colonialism, but more often, the narrators of these poems are made aware of their cultural difference, as in the poem "scraps of paper":

> the sudden silences when he enters rooms
> his brown face alone stands out
> the furtive looks, whispers about men in long hair.

In this poem, the narrator turns to his writing as a response to this sense of isolation and judgment, creating "memories on scraps of paper" as a way of asserting and validating Indigenous presence in these "small towns and villages / dying under the prairie sky." If the writer here is a lone wolf, he is also the one who knows how to use stories to survive.

A very different iteration of the wolf in these poems is the creature of urban sociality and celebration, as represented most clearly in the blues ethos of Mercredi's fourth book, *Duke of Windsor: Wolf Sings the Blues*. Titled after a popular Winnipeg blues bar and Indigenous meeting place, this book is alive with the rhythms and themes of the blues, drawing upon African-American traditions of lament, resistance, and community solidarity. In this context, it seems more than possible that *mahikan ka onot* is a Cree/Métis incarnation of Howlin' Wolf, the famous bluesman who adapted Mississippi Delta blues into the urban context of 1950s Chicago, and transformed American music in the process. One of Howlin' Wolf's great contributions was to bring the rural Black sensibility of Delta blues into an urban, electrified milieu, reflecting a new mode of Black empowerment that came into being in the era of The Great Migration. Thus it is no surprise that Chicago blues was enormously attractive to Duncan Mercredi and many other Indigenous people who moved to the cities in the 1960s and '70s. Duncan's poetry attempts a similar fusion of gritty urban life with traditional stories and life on the land. As he writes in "yesterday's song,"

> even though my feet are concrete hardened
> and my spirit tells stories of neon and blues
> i am the son of muskeg and spruce
> i still dance to the music of yesterday.

The final kind of wolf that haunts this book is the Roogaroo, the character so prominent in the Métis oral stories that Duncan learned from his kookum. As I mentioned above, the Roogaroo is capable of changing from wolf to human form, usually at will. It is often shunned in polite society or associated with mysterious or destabilizing forces, including the powers of women. At the same time, many Roogaroo stories also show a strong sympathy for this character—so much so that the Roogaroo can be seen as an oft-misunderstood Métis culture hero in works like Maria Campbell's "Roogaroos" and Cherie Dimaline's *Empire of Wild*. In Duncan Mercredi's own oral stories, the Roogaroo is sometimes a beautiful young woman, sometimes an old lady, sometimes an indeterminate shape that leaves canine tracks in the snow. It seems to be capable of time travel, and it reflects our own selves back to us when we gaze at it. Always in these stories, the Roogaroo is the core of a mystery that the audience is asked to solve. To me this is reminiscent of the many appearances of *mahikanuk* in this book. The wolf is never presented as an explanation or a straightforward symbol in these poems, but instead it arrives as a witness and as an embodiment of mystery, an invitation for readers to ponder their own place in relation to the story. *mahikan* is watching us with its otherworldly eyes as we explore the meaning of the poem. Perhaps it is even testing us.

—*Warren Cariou*

Notes

1. For detailed discussion of the effects of the dam upon Misipawistik, see Waldram (1988) and Neckoway (2018).
2. Statistics Canada reports that in the 2016 Census, "867,415 Aboriginal people lived in a metropolitan area of at least 30,000 people, accounting for over half (51.8%) of the total Aboriginal population." https://www150.statcan.gc.ca/n1/daily-quotidien/171025/dq171025a-eng.htm

Works Cited

Campbell, Maria, trans. *Stories of the Road Allowance People*. Revised edition. Saskatoon: Gabriel Dumont Institute Press, 2010.

Cariou, Warren. "Indigenous Literature and Other Verbal Arts, Canada (1960–2012)." In Daniel Heath Justice and James Cox, eds., *The Oxford Handbook of Indigenous American Literature*. Oxford: Oxford University Press, 2014.

Dimaline, Cherie. *Empire of Wild*. Toronto: Random House, 2019.

Neckoway, Ramona. "'Where the Otters Play,' 'Horseshoe Bay,' 'Footprint' and Beyond: Spatial and Temporal Considerations of Hydroelectric Energy Production in Northern Manitoba." PhD dissertation, University of Manitoba, 2018.

Statistics Canada. www150.statcan.gc.ca.

Waldram, James. *As Long as the Rivers Run: Hydroelectric Development and Native Communities in Western Canada*. Winnipeg: University of Manitoba Press, 1988.

Other Resources

Beeds, Tasha. "Remembering the Poetics of Ancient Sound kistêsinâw/wîsahkêcâhk's maskihkiy (Elder Brother's Medicine)." In Neal McLeod, ed., *Indigenous Poetics in Canada*. Waterloo: Wilfrid Laurier University Press, 2014, 61–71.

Mercredi, Duncan. "Achimo." In Neal McLeod, ed., *Indigenous Poetics in Canada*. Waterloo: Wilfrid Laurier University Press, 2014, 17–22.

——. "Writing and Life." In Paul DePasquale, Renate Eigenbrod, and Emma LaRocque, eds., *Across Cultures / Across Borders: Canadian Aboriginal and Native American Literature*. Peterborough, ON: Broadview Press, 2009, 125–26.

Minor, Michael. "Decolonizing through Poetry in the Indigenous Prairie Context." PhD dissertation, University of Manitoba, 2016.

Spirit of the Wolf
(for Livie)

      silently
            she slips
                  out of the shadows

  raising
      her head
           she sings
                a
                  song
                  to
                   the
                  dark
                  moon

A Remembering Smile

I walk the streets
   full of strangers with eyes distant
   unseeing
faces cold against concrete walls
   but
   once in a while my eyes go distant
I remember and I smile, a secret smile
   a remembering smile

Recalling happier times
   long time ago
   distant
still hearing the river
   the river wild and free
   alive

My nookum* still skinned rabbits and squirrels
   with hands gnarled and scarred
   from too many winters
still,
   they were gentle hands
that soothed burning fevers

Winters were cold
   children wrapped tight against the wind
   still, we played all day
having to be called in at sunset
   sitting in front of the hot tin stove
   fire red from the heat warming my feet
sharing nookum's tea

Spring, the river breaks free
   loud, ice crackling like rifle fire
   we lie awake at nights listening
imagination caught up in the story I tell
   about the war raging on the river
   all laugh when I am done
we snuggle into the warmth of the feather blanket
   little brother the warmest in the middle

Summer, hot, river alive with laughter
   young brown bodies dot the clear blue water
   some standing naked on the shore
trembling with cold
   a breeze whispers gently in my ear
while an eagle rides the sky above me

Fall, the sound of geese in the night sky
   singing a good-bye song
   as only they can sing
good-bye, good-bye, we shall never forget

I wake to a light snowfall
   and the concrete forest that surrounds me
   begins to awaken
I ride the escalator with a remembering smile
   while others watch me curiously
   with fear, I wonder
So I whistle an almost forgotten tune
   good-bye, good-bye
         We shall never ...

---

*   Author's note: nookum is a possessive form, meaning "my grandmother". kookum is more like "everyone's grandmother."

Broken Glass

A spirit cries within me
crying for release,
I slam the door,
placing a lock on it.
The spirit's voice is left,
crying softly through the ages.
Visions visit my dreams,
people on the other side call.
I drain another bottle,
washing away accusing eyes.
They scream in fear,
alcohol burns their souls.
I shut my eyes and ears,
their agony is not mine.
They whisper tales of glory,
I shake my head clear, their stories are not mine.
But a spirit cries within me,
weaker, yet still fighting a sightless man.
Spirit attempts to lead a blind warrior
on a journey over broken glass.

scraps of paper

he carries his memories on scraps of paper
scattered among his clothes in his battered bag
that has travelled his journeys
through small towns and villages
dying under the prairie sky
pieces of lives etched in the headings of his mind
treherne hotel, friendship is our business
bottomless cups, home fries, perogies, boiled not fried
george's Chinese menu in emerson, enjoyed by farmers
and americans across the line
helen, walking, always moving, in a sing song voice
soup's hot, it's good, yeah, good food, real Chinese
then
the sudden silences when he enters rooms
his brown face alone stands out
the furtive looks, whispers about men in long hair
quick departures and shy smiles from children
before their chairs are flung around - don't stare
nervous parents chide
chilly looks from grandfather types
grandmothers move restless in their chairs
watching the door
then
late at night listening to the jukebox
in the bar beneath him, shaking the floor and bed
he writes his memories on scraps of paper
to the beat of rock and roll and the national
playing a back drop song
then
he lies down on a bed like many others
he hears the same voices everywhere
only the faces have changed
but they all look alike on the scraps of paper
he writes on
then
he sleeps and dreams of little towns and villages
dying under a prairie sky
their names on scraps of paper scattered among his clothes

mask

oh, canada, thy true face is revealed
as your mask is torn off your face
by our people desperate to be seen and heard
as we sink standing on a raft of promises

oh, canada, we see your face and it is evil
burning effigies in visions that cross your mind
itching fingers when you pass us by
dirty money to children with no future
for your own quick relief
then screaming your hate to your children
about the money taken from you to support
the bums
you kiss them goodnight with the smell of a young child
on your breath
then you phone the radio to vent your rage and hate
oh, canada, thy true face is revealed
oh, canada, thy true face is hatred

as the walls came up

i went wandering one night in my dreams
i travelled on concrete rivers
choked with people
seeking sun and silence

i travelled east and saw hope rising
behind a line of guns
and i saw a wall come down
i saw the world cheer and raise hands high
in victory

i travelled west and saw money
piled high as the sky
blanketing the sun
darkening hearts with greed

i travelled south to burning jungles
and saw my brothers struggle to reclaim the rivers
only to fall and fade away
as the world watched and shook their heads

i travelled north and saw barricades
with women and children standing guard
watching a country burning effigies
and hearing a nation cheer

i woke to find i stood behind iron bars
with my brothers and sisters
alone against the tide of hate
and in the distance i heard the gates slam shut
against the wings of the eagle
clipping its freedom
i cried
as the walls came up

the final solution

in the early evening
as the sun readies for bed
and the moon is still invisible
in the early dusk
i feel its call as it strums the song
in my heart
a song full of sorrow, anger and fear
as i watch a people alone
behind manmade barricades
making a stand
against invisible walls
that stretch from sea to sea
and a sheet of white covers the land
dotted with burning effigies
as people dance around them
mocking a nation with their hate
the final solution is at hand
shades of Hitler's brothers holding
in their hands a maple leaf and fleur de lis
with a sign behind them reading
HERE HAVE SOME KOOL-AID
IT'LL MAKE YOUR DREAMS COME TRUE
AND THE PAIN WILL BE SHORT BUT SWEET
the world watches in wonder
as a mask of a nation is peeled away
and its beauty is only a cover

Mothers

mothers of this land we seek forgiveness
we the protectors of your gifts

we have failed as there is hunger
wars rage and children die

children with bellies distended
cry at night with a hunger
a hunger for food and love

we do not provide for we are busy
busy with fighting useless wars
we deny others our food
knowledge is withheld
others could use it on us

oh mothers we have forsaken your trust
trust that you gave when this world was born
to protect the land
to care for the children
to forever treasure what you have taught
to be faithful to all

oh mothers we have shamed you
we have used you
we have abused you
now we discard you

mothers
we ask forgiveness
we who have nothing

you have taken it all back

Gabriel (Buffalo Hunt)

Sound of thunder under a clear blue sky
prairie grass bends in the wind

Ground trembles under your feet
rumbling sound stirs your soul
eagerly you mount your horse

For over the hill the sound is louder
closer and closer it comes
so you ride to the thunder
and the sight never ceases to amaze you

Brown, moving brown thundering across the plains
dust blocks the sun, an orange ball in the sky
and as the mass moves closer it blackens the sky

A moving mass of muscle and brawn
large heads held low to the ground
tongues lolling, eyes wild as the wind

Brown brothers ride amongst these beasts
darting in and out of the way
"Yip, yip, yip," they yell firing into the herd
you see the flash of powder and later a popping sound
a beast crumbles to the ground
smell of blood in the air

So ride Gabriel the hunt is on
and into this living moving thunder you ride
the black horse you're on is one with you

Grasping your rifle you load on the run
firing and loading, reins in your teeth
never wasting a shot, bison drop around you

A riderless horse thunders by eyes wild with fear
caught in this moving nightmare
so ride Gabriel the hunt is on

10 / *mahikan ka onot*

Your horse stumbles beneath you
grabbing the reins you lift his head
out of the crowd you move
"Yi, yi, yi," you yell, "out of my way
I do not die out here."
With the strength of ten you turn your horse
so ride Gabriel the hunt is on

Heart swelling with excitement
from the smell of dust and gun powder
you ride beside the moving herd
out of shot you ride for the thrill

Brown brothers of saddleless horses
with bow and arrow they hunt, fly by you
arrows finding their marks
so ride Gabriel the hunt is on

Miles and miles you ride following the herd
till your horse stumbles throwing you off
you hit the ground running laughter in your eyes
"Yi, yi, yi," you yell
the herd turns away from you
leaving you standing alone in the darkening prairie sky
so ride Gabriel the hunt is on

At the end of day you head to camp
counting fallen buffalo that women and children skin
dogs fighting over scraps, coyotes stealing unguarded meat

Women tending broken bodies soothing mourning wives
campfires dot the prairie as far as you can see
So ride Gabriel this could be the last hunt
For white fences are moving west

mahikan (Wolf)

Silent as day falling into night
he glides across fresh fallen snow
barely leaving a trail in the land
like a shadow in the night
he blends in the dark landscape

a movement on the ground catches his attention
he stops, body quivering with excitement
a rabbit frozen with fear suddenly bolts
mahikan jumps to the chase

zig-zagging across the frozen ground
the two hurtle through the silent woods
mahikan never misses the rabbit's turns
he could lunge and snap the rabbit's neck
but he waits

rabbit stumbles burying his face in the snow
quivering eyes full of fear he awaits his death
mahikan's eyes yellow expressionless stop
he howls at the moon, a mournful cry
his cry is answered in the wind

he trots away, glancing back only once
he is not hungry tonight
the run was only for the joy of life

Forgotten Words

He stands up there this old man
  white hair long, hung in braids
Struggling to talk in broken Cree
  he stutters and pauses
He explains why he talks like he does

As a child he spent time in a boarding school
  losing what little he had gained
Strapped for speaking his tongue
  he grew up with foreign words

A stranger in his land he wandered
  searching for his place in life
Accepted nowhere but in a bottle
  lost for years in a land of lost spirits

He wandered alone nothing to guide him
  until the cry of the fiddle and the beat of a drum
Drew him into the circle
  filled with many faces like his

The sadness breaks as he sits
feels peace embracing him
He listens
and dances

Forgotten words emerge
slowly
Painfully he tells his story
as the circle makes him one

Betty

Betty, who heard your screams that night
a gentle man, a family man, a silent man
a respected man

walking home, no cares in the world
glad to be alive
a car pulls up full of young men
four looking for an easy time

Young men who'd heard stories
about easy dark-haired girls
they force you into their car
but you fight

Betty who heard your screams that night
a gentle man, a family man, a silent man,
a respected man

Bruised, battered, you struggled on
out of town they drove
in a well known car
but you fought because to give in
would be giving in to ignorance
what was yours was to be saved not used
by ignorant men
who'd heard stories of dark-haired girls

Betty who heard your screams that night
a gentle man, a family man, a silent man
a respected man

Clothes ripped you fought on
only with will and pride you fought
these men who thought that by virtue of their color
you were theirs to use

Betty who heard your screams that night
a gentle man, a family man, a silent man
a respected man

14 / *mahikan ka onot*

Dragged through the snow, naked body bloodied
still you cursed them and you prayed
did you pray to a white god
one that did not hear

did their rage finally explode
at one stronger than them
did you watch the flash from their weapon
as the lights of the car reflected off it
did you count the blows before the pain overcame you
did you hear them laugh as they left
did one turn around and did you see remorse
they'd heard stories of dark-haired girls after all

Betty who heard your screams that night
silent now as the blood from your body reddened the white
snow around you

Betty who heard your screams that night
a town heard your screams that night
then turned its back on truth

years pass and a province hears your screams
they turn off the lights

years pass and a country hears your screams
and they pull the blankets over their heads
and sleep

A Gathering

I saw a gathering of eagles
high
circling the sun
dancing

I saw a gathering of wolves
running
across pure snow
singing
to a winter's moon

I saw a gathering of people
together
in a circle
as one
dancing

I saw a gathering of effigies
burning
in the distance
eerily
blood red against a purple black sky

I saw a gathering of white vultures
watching
the burning effigies
approvingly
as helpless people danced in the flames

I went to a gathering
no one was there

Black Robe

oh black robe
why do you kneel in front of me
who do you pray to
as you fumble with my clothes
are those beads of sweat on your forehead
or my tears of shame
at your desire
or your impatience
at my tears that
appear

oh black robe
your sighs of pleasure paralyze me
i stand in terror and hurt
as you pray and handle me
i ache inside as your god turns his back
ignoring my shame

oh black robe
is this sin yours
or mine

i feel used
dirty

this is not what you preach on sundays

dreams of the wolf in the city

dreams of the wolf in the city
disturbed by passing cars and sirens
dangers hidden under manicured lawns
cutting feet of children
who play with discarded needles and used condoms
wolf watches from his safe house
unseen
till he hits the streets at midnight
watching strangers avert their eyes
fearful of the wolf that walks upright
and the dangers he poses
are only stories told to children
and they dream of the wolf in the city

wolf's hackles rise on his back
and he growls in his sleep
till his dreams take him to the land of northern lights
and he hears the creaking of his kookum's chair
and the coolness of her hand on his fevered brow
wolf sighs in his dream and tears appear
as he watches a casket lowered into the earth
full of needle marks and stripped bare of trees
earth mother trembles beneath wolf's feet
and he feels anguish
wolf runs as he feels the breath of diesel monsters
and the forest turns to concrete under his feet
and trails turn to back alleys

the sounds of breaking glass and curses
and someone's pain wakens him to the sound of an alarm
fred beside him sleeps on
unaware of his restless dreams
wolf stumbles to his feet
struggling to light a cigarette
to calm his nerves
and he sings softly to himself
it is but a dream and I live it only at night
wolf shudders at this thought
and he walks into the day

and the fears of the strangers in daylight's brightness
are magnified in newspaper headlines
dreams of the wolf in the city are real

crazy face junior gone wild

i met them on a greed day in a strange place full of
contradictions
and skin heads with twelve eyes slam dancing to the blues
suits and ties were doing grand theft canoe disguised as
week-end cowboys in their creased never dirty blue jeans
sort of bent out of shape with bullet proof vests
facing working girls taking a break between transactions
straw hatted leather jackets with work scarred hands
face a duck shot hunter with a voice of boom holding back
red tied jawboned snow dogs screaming about bat sweat and
that honest john wasn't so honest and the intruders were
insane who had rats for friends
crazy face junior walks in and red necks sit and take notice
while making eyes at the man dressed as a woman licks
his/her red lips while caressing the young man through his
jeans imagining his first blow job
while playing pool then pontius pilate flies in with his
seven dwarfs
singing about no more fear hate white power luke cries
on albert street quoting scriptures and 18:9-14 written
on alley walls
seven dwarfs laugh as they take his bible and read the
name of the motel inside the pages of luke's bible
he claimed from the motel desk of some forgotten one horse
town an afterthought crazy face junior had heard on his
travels and he'd keep the lights on all night trying to
keep white collar at bay by wrapping himself in his blankets
even when the night was hot and he kept the windows and
bathroom door closed pontius pilate grabs and crazy face
junior goes wild and screams about the death of the white
race and crazy face junior gone wild tells the seven dwarfs
he was sure he saw jesus on a bike on some back road one
day
then he tells them of meeting me in a back alley reading
walls and finding dr. hook towing back alleys looking for
the iron maiden while dodging piss-filled potholes
scaring drunks scaring me waiting for the light to change
on portage and smith catching the looks by fake haired men
and the devil i meet is named crazy face junior gone wild

who dodges my shadow and i see a flicker of doubt in his
eyes when i say hi crazy face junior gone wild makes the
sign of the cross at this pony tailed torn jacketed indian
wearing a purse
i walk into the albert and i see crazy face junior gone wild
talking to the seven dwarfs with suckers
and suspect devices
in their hands led by pontius pilate who says to them i dub
thee unimportant and crazy face junior goes wild before me
and tells me duck shot hunter will find me on fat tuesday
down at the albert but i'm not worried jesus lizard walks
beside me

Lake Winnipeg 1956

parents rise before the dawn
waking me to the sounds of pots and pans
and quiet conversation
while the wind begins to blow
the sudden barking of the dogs heralds the arrival
of the Bombardier

idling outside, it waits
i watch my father through the frost covered window
enter the day
the dogs rise expectantly
shaking the cold off eager to run
growling at the machine that has changed their lives
and eased their burden
my father disappears into the dark pre-dawn

highway 75 1991

30 below outside and i hear the wind begin to rise
i struggle awake and into my clothes
the voice on the radio tells me to dress warm
and i shiver in the dark room
bear begins to rise as i drink my coffee
he wants out
i listen to the sound of the wind
hoping against hope that the day is lost
it's 30 below and the city begins to wake

Lake Winnipeg 1956

the wind always blows on the lake
with no protection the wind bites at exposed skin
the horizon stretching into a vast whiteness
of the lake and reaches upwards to meet the sky
eyes burn from the glare of the sun and snow
minds feelings long replaced by boredom
clothes frozen and mitts caked with ice
the day stretches into the night
and the body begins to sag
under the weight of the cold

highway 75 1991

the wind has gotten stronger and we travel snow covered roads
straining our eyes trying to glimpse the road
as the wind chases behind us rattling the van
but we're safely cocooned inside
we peer through the blowing snow
all we can see is the line of trees ghostly in the distance
the day begins to darken and i think of my father
i hear the challenge from the past that calls me

Lake Winnipeg 1956 highway 75 1991

i slump on the chair exhausted cold
i nod off

                        my father enters
                        still covered in ice

i watch through the past as he undresses
hanging his clothes over the stove
mine are scattered over the floor

               my father always has supper by himself
                          eating in silence
                            fatigue on his
                            wind burned face

i collapse on the bed
face burning from the wind
i listen to the silence of my room
and i see the lake through my father's eyes
the empty vastness stretching forever
much like the highways i work on
the lake and highway join
becoming one

                        i doze and dream
              i am covered in ice and i eat in silence
                   i have become my father

the sun rises red

see the sun rise in the east
hear the call of the wolves
as they seek a place to rest
i stand on a hill
looking for you in the sky
but the sunshine blinds my eyes
and the wolves' songs deafen my hearing
so i can't follow the sound of your voice
calling me

calling me from the past
to tell our stories to the world
but the world has closed their minds
and see only what they want to see
and so they hunt us down
to silence our truths
and i hear you calling me
but my weakness brings me down

i drag my weary body down the hill
and i seek a place to sleep
but all the doors are closed to me
all the people have gone deaf

and don't hear the knock upon their doors
i curse the ones that gave them help
to let them live among us
as we watched them push us to the brink
and let us straddle the edge of death
then blame us for their sins

the wolves' songs have gotten weaker
all the rivers have died
and the sun rises red each morning
and the air is not fit to breathe
so we stand idly by
waiting for another drink
to drown our tears and pain
to blind us to the scene

of young bodies beneath
the cancer that walks this land
holding his hand out to help
instead he pushes us over the edge
and the last sound we hear
is the sound of cheering
across this land

three in the morning

        a cigarette a cold beer a typewriter
          three in the morning
can't sleep
      going through withdrawal
          no sweet smoke to ease the dreams

         i sit and stare
         no sound
      flickering lights behind my eyes
        nothing happens
i can hear every creak of the floor
bear grunts in the back room
the sound of music from my daughter's room

         fred sleeps on
         but she's restless
      does she sense my troubled mind
        do i intrude into her dream state
intermittent traffic sounds from portage avenue
rouse me
cigarette is out
unsmoked
the beer is warm
and the typewriter is cold
i resign myself to my fate
and collapse on the couch
letting my dreams take me where they want
i let go and fly

fort and york

i wander these back streets
seeking the music of the night
reaching the corner of fort and york
just this side of midnight

i come to the place
where men seek men
to play in the dark
hiding their shame in back alleys

i hear the wailing of Dave's harp
cutting through the night
and the stench of the street

i dance by myself
looking for the castle
and time changes
to near two in the morning
and the blue note holds court
with puppies learning the tunes
of my youth

i stumble over the garbage
waking the man who sleeps by his food
he asks me if i have the answer
but his voice is lost
in the night
drowned out by the scream of the siren
and the roar of the gun
broken glass rains down on us from above
as angry words are exchanged between invisible lovers

the moon fades behind the windy corners
tall concrete trees
and he asks me again for the answer
but i leave him with nothing
but empty glasses he tips back

and i hear young lovers
fumble in doorways
seeking the key to rooms
where they dream of release
from the dawn
here in the heart of fort and york
just this side of daylight

something you said

it could be anything

  the way someone laughs
  or the scent of a certain perfume
  i can never remember the name
maybe when i'm just starting to wake
  and i'll reach beside me
  to the empty side of the motel bed
  but i feel the warmth of you
sometimes it's a song
  it was our song
  when we were young
  and we'd walk outside
  to a night full of stars
  and the song would follow behind us
it could be anything
  a whisper, a cough,
  or the way your breath would catch
  like that time we saw mountains
  riding in that train
  racing the sun to the ocean
sometimes the smell of sweetgrass
  will find you walking beside me
  like we did last summer
  united across this country
  and i could see the pride
  in your eyes
and i'll smile
  maybe just before i fall asleep
  and i'll hear a whisper
  just before i close my eyes
  and the words i hear
  will be words of love
  and i'll smile again
  and whisper back
  as my words catch the breeze
  carrying my message to your land of dreams
it could be anything
  but it's not
  it's love

strangers

still

    no matter what we've been through together
    the long nights
    tipping back cold ones
    under a winter sky
    a billion stars above us
    listening to the wolves around us
    encircling us like brothers

still

    no matter what we've been through together
    lighting smokes
    sharing j's
    and lies
    listening to rock and blues
    on the radio

still

    no matter what we've been through together
    hearing about the troubles at home
    and what a bitch life is
    and boy is it cold out today
    too cold to work
    but we don't stop
    even as our piss freezes as it hits the ground
    we go on

still

    no matter what we've been through together
    laughing at bad jokes we tell
    while lying in bunk beds
    about four hundred miles from home
    stoned out of our heads
    and feeling every bump on the old mattress
    and the coldness of the trailer
    seeps under the blanket
    cursing at the isolation of the bush

still
> we shared bottles
> watching the sun rise
> as it began its day's journey
> we'd laugh at the absurdity of life
> as if we knew it all

friends

yet
yet despite all we've been through together
> you are still a stranger to me

Sandilands

not much to see in this sandy soil
laid bare by smoke belching noise polluting
heavy machinery
scarring the land
tearing the roots of trees out of the ground
protesting loudly as they fall

lines crisscross its pine covered face
visible only from above
while roads stretch for miles in every direction
heading for nowhere from nowhere

and in its pine depths
below the branches
where it's cool on hot summer days
patchy sunlight filters through the trees
catching the dew on spider webs
like diamonds glinting across the forest floor
the soft hum of flies lulling me to sleep
then the sudden buzz of fear as they're caught
in beauty

i stretch as i rise
stepping over plastic bags, aluminum cans
broken beer bottles
old no trespassing signs nailed on trees
faded from an unknown number of seasons
so old i trespass just to read the letters
spotting old house foundations
overgrown with weeds and willows
locking its memories in their roots
discarded tires lean against rotted stumps
housing a family of mice

villages appear out of nowhere
cut out of the forest wilderness
neat yards nestled against the jumbled abandoned
houses
as the old people watch them die
year by year
fighting the shifting sands
and leaning precariously against the winds
that whistle and whisper on winter nights

they wonder where the children's laughter has gone
while they visit the dead in graveyards overgrown with weeds
life, death returning to the earth once more
becoming part of the cycle
dust to dust

wolf and shadows

what are you becoming brown warrior
is it another ride you seek
taking you away from past sins
you think   but   the days stretch into another ride
to where
what are you becoming brown warrior
after you lost the trail
on city streets and back alleys
full of shadows and blues
oh   how they tempted you with that back
alley song and neon lights
did you see this vision as a child
through spruce boughs and shadows
brown warrior

traditional smoke

you can have your fake beads and furs
you can dance to a broken drum for tourists
you can talk about peace and understanding
cleansing yourself with sweetgrass
and crawling into the womb of a sweatlodge
seeking visions and salvations
while at the same time you dream of ways to exploit
this gift

but not me
i hang out with traditional smoke
people with nothing but tobacco to offer
so you cross the street to avoid eye contact
might get infected and you brag of your children's blood
and the strength they get from this blood that flows in them
and you forget about traditional smoke
it won't make you rich

traditional smoke people don't lie to me
offering as a gift the last of what they may have
expecting nothing in return but friendship
they will not dance to a discordant drum
or enter the sweatlodge womb
while they conspire against another
they do not wash with sweetgrass smoke
and pray to the directions
while plotting inside their minds to use their gifts
to gain favor inside the white god's house
traditional smoke people don't dance to the thunder eagle's song
for themselves

36 / *mahikan ka onot*

blue collar blues

i miss working with men
with their beliefs hanging over their belts
sun booze scarred faces and nicotine stained
bodies stretched into clothes
smelling of yesterday
eyes red rimmed
nervously looking inward
trying to see back to last night
after the lights went out
glimpsing flashing lights
passed around in the dark
head hanging retching echoes
bruised skins and scarred elbows
tattooed arms in the latest rug burn
insane laughter
driving without lights
on some northern road
acting like we were in the wild west
strutting in
stumbling out
yelling obscenities at the woman
laying you down with one backhand
someone laughing picking us up
two hours before daybreak
was that just yesterday
i knew these men
who looked at me and wondered
we crossed each others' lives
but we never stayed
i miss working with these men

statue*

oh bent naked mis-shapen spokesman of god
with nothing to cover your shame
but half built circles to hide you from the cold
faced away from the river that gave your kookum life
now discarded by your descendants
with some ill-conceived notion of greatness
oh bastard child of the prairies
whipped and beaten by time and myth
placed on a pedestal made of leather and bones
bleached white by the prairie wind and sun
gaunt body holding grotesque head
writhing in pain
forever and ever
in mind's eye we see lies that were told
revealed now in your anguish
staring in vain at the doors in front of you
they remain closed
but one of you sits in the queen's house
shoulder to shoulder
with one like them that draped the noose around your neck
a brother of the wind
rejecting the past
as though you were pre-ordained to serve your enemies
oh discarded child of the prairies
the wind carries your message
but no one hears the agony of defeat
the weight of years lost standing naked
ridicule heavy on your twisted shoulders
insane he spoke to spirits
but we understood
oh abused man of god
the tears have not stopped
your sons have discarded the leather and tobacco
trading them for a bible and collar
that binds you to a vengeful god
leaving your children to wander for a century
still seeking their place
while hiding a part of themselves
savages

you too lived inside leather houses
you slept on buffalo robes
now the pain of rejection by two nations
is etched in your body
mis-shapen man of the prairies
you hold your head high
on a false pedestal
your circle is incomplete
what was your dream

---

* The statue described here is Marcien Lemay's sculpture of Louis Riel as a nude figure, which was displayed on the Manitoba Legislature grounds until 1990, when it was moved because of public concern that it was not a respectful depiction. The statue is now situated on the grounds of L'Université de Saint-Boniface, largely hidden from public view by two large semicircular barriers.

spring

  slipping into the river in my dreams
   when it would wake in the spring
    ignoring the chill of spring
     i would dive into its depth
      to cleanse myself of winter's grip
       bursting out of its embrace
        renewal

  after the stories were put away
   laid to rest in my heart and mind
    i would wander the river
     searching for signs of life
      waiting for the return of music
       that would travel the wind
        from the south
         rebirth

tripping back

it's always a trip back
looking north
city sky fading behind me
taking a glance at my youth
the scent of hide and cedar
peat moss stuffed logs
white washed sun faded
houses lining the river
stumbling on the path i had taken
still tripping
on seen and unseen deadfalls
scraping the same memories
of pain and joy
etched on a faded cross
unable to face the promises
i made and broke
a thousand times
to too many strangers
now faceless
i can't remember your name
though you enter my dreams
when i glance back
i glimpse your smile
city

eagle woman sky flyer (revised)*

eagle woman sky flyer
dancing on summer breezes
drawing invisible patterns against the sky
                do you dream
as you soar above me
silent as the northern lights
that brightened my northern sky
                do you sing
where i lay as a child
watching you fly above me
i was a man/child when you first appeared
                do you remember
eagle woman sky flyer
i begged you to take me
but you couldn't hear me
                do you mourn
the death of a young one
burned by the wires that hum between us
strung between metal trees
                do you weep
as my song comes to an end
and my voice has changed
now i hum the melody
for the words are now only a memory

eagle woman sky flyer
take me
my path is unclear
full of hidden traps
temptations
easy to lose oneself in the night
eagle woman sky flyer
they offer me nothing
only promises
like before
still
they circle the wagons in their minds
and the church stands guard
protecting the sinners
eagle woman sky flyer
the child only plays at night
coming out from the last door
around the last corner of my heart
eagle woman sky flyer
i want to see the sun

---

* The first version of this poem was performed on CBC Radio in the summer of 1990, during the Oka crisis. The revised version reproduced here was written about two weeks later.

where dreams begin

where dreams begin
inside a mother's womb
listening to the drum beat of her heart
and the gentle sounds of water
life giver

the rustle of leaves outside the window
a block from city traffic
children's voices drifting in
skipping along on music that i hear
on a summer night

dozing
trying to catch my dreams
kookum rocking in her chair
rattle of dishes
aroma of fresh bannock
mothers calling children inside
and the singing river in the background

where dreams begin
a memory awakens
the barking of the dogs
the slap of waves against the boat
rocking gently on the lake

sounds of sirens
wake me
and i can feel the baby inside you
struggling to see the place
where dreams begin

street poetry

red style rez style
indian territory
inner city red terror
as portrayed on city evening news
innuendo rumour filled myths
a nightmare from the past
and still they circle
greying seagulls in fancy cars
smelling slightly old world
picking up pieces standing on the corner
leaving a few more shards scattered on the sidewalk
lost souls working for a quick trip
out of their lives

pow wow jiving driving man
caught in a drum beat song
riding wave after wave of tobacco smoke
caressing a sweet grass sage scented woman
strutting striding turning heads
catching her secret smile
maybe it was a trick of the light
or an active imagination and wishful dreaming
but i thought i caught a wink
making a street poetry man dance

blue collar stained sunbaked windburned working face
hey buck get a haircut
reverberating throughout the southern reaches
left echoing in little deathbed watched towns
stamped on his back the mark of cain
and another word flung out of passing cars lands
and is filed away with all the rest of those silent trips
inside his mind images of yesterday criss-crossed with railway tracks
humming hydro lines and back trails full of muskeg and water
remembering each line cut by the callouses on his hands
and a memory is stored
every muscle and joint aching with each recall

street poetry
red style rez style
long haired four directions man
draws another photograph thought buried
recalling the crying tree falling
spirit territory
an image an idea a vision
i could see the past in the rings of the moon
no one no one
even rez time blues lovers
can understand my story
while trying to analyse written thoughts
with european assimilated english use
i dream in cree and north
smelling of muskeg, spruce and cedar
my fire burns into this land i stand on
from birth to death
to death to life
a circle never ending
i have nowhere else to go
my path leads not from the east or west
but from the sky
an eagle cries my story
street poetry
red rez style

nine streets past crazy

nine streets past crazy
still can recognize a blast from the past
leaning against the maclaren
waiting as we always did for an offer
selling laughter for a beer on cool saturday afternoons
looking with it strolling down main
ignoring the piss on the sidewalk
neatly sidestepping teetering friday night people
making that move seen at the arena
score
saved a loonie
just nine streets past crazy
all boarded up and dying
a friend lost blood there
going out to visit
stepped into a knife instead
left a stain on the carpet
and in my heart
just an empty space
nine streets past crazy
on a saturday morning
walking with sixty
nursing a hangover
what year was that
the Brunswick had go-go girls
my dad went to see
after a long drive from grand rapids
on dust covered roads
a back seat full of kids
travelling at the speed of our screams
just nine streets past crazy
watching all day movies for a buck
stepping into nightday
street alive with brown
wide-eyed from the north
just nine streets past crazy
sitting in the darkest corner
underaged hiding in the shadows
saturday evenings

rolling drunks in the back
c-weed was beginning at the brunswick
and we'd go downstairs
into wall to wall brown
dancing
what year was that
nine streets past crazy
heard the gunshot and the rage
on open line radios
white on red on black on yellow
refusing to see from outside their skins
believing in their infallibility
and in their laws as divine
just nine streets past crazy
watching wondering
counting the number of times i was turned away
from the good street
i wandered into after losing my way
nine streets past crazy

snowbound

it's been a long ride on a bad road
made worse by unexplained detours
appearing on blind trails
snowbound
held hostage by myself and a bad road
caught in a time warp
in some northern camp
next to nowhere
and dammed up rivers
going nowhere to feed the south

snowbound
in between lifers
that made the trip and never came down
whispering to invisible companions
sitting at separate tables
inching closer to themselves
when they see you walk in
a stranger in a strange place
made stranger by lifers
still dressed in their very best polyester pants
flashback
to the city
lowtrack walking
cruising the strip
for a quick one nighter

snowbound
on a very bad road
caught in a three vehicle traffic jam
behind gardewine north
and an impatient bootlegger
trying to beat the storm to the bar
watching the end of the day approaching

snowbound
on a very bad road
not picturing the trail ahead
only the relative smoothness
of a very rough road behind us

howl

all i want to do is howl
when i look back
and find out
they're gaining
but i have nothing left to say
to them
that came suddenly
silently flying on water
with shiny gifts and pretty beads
full of promises
and a black book that listed our sins
them that came suddenly
breaking every rule their god had laid down
though shalt have no other gods
but he was invisible
so he was forgotten and left to wither
becoming dust through the ages

and

another legend was born
a legend of nobody
living without false dreams
and knowing his limitations
would disappear into himself
from time to time
until one day
he forgot to return
and now his body
abandoned
sits in the corner
at the end of a sterile corridor
and his message deemed unacceptable
due to the volatility of the times
gathers dust

we are wolf

we are wolf
hunted to near extinction
driven deeper into our past
hidden in shadows
forced to dance in secret
to a silent drum
lying in wait
in tiny spaces
set apart to be changed
unable to shape ourselves
in our past image
white on brown or death
our reward
for being here
when others arrived
we are wolf
a price on our heads
judged by old world laws
by strangers with tainted gifts
who fled the injustice
and persecution
to pass it down on us
we gave our permission
to live side by side
watching our side lose
and places were removed
piece by piece
and invisible walls rose
to the sky
we looked and howled
in anger
we are wolf
we are restless

vision quest

must have strayed too far off the path
tripping over the same words as before
circled around till i came upon myself
still lost
i guess i lied
when i told that story
but it seemed so real at the time
but you found me out
and ignored me when i passed by you
even as i rambled on
trying to make it right
must have strayed too far off the path
unable to penetrate the darkness
closing in around me
hiding you on the trail

i could dream in Cree one time
my visions full of music kookum sang
echoing from the past
now it's all jumbled and lost
among concrete canyons
full of exhaust and used smells
must have strayed too far off the path
for now i dream in white
inside city lights
the colour of youth misplaced
inside plastic bags
inhaled in back alleys
new visions manufactured by lies
struggling to find my feet
staring blankly at the setting sun
not knowing the direction i was going
or remembering the nature of the path behind me

52 / *mahikan ka onot*

on this day

on this day of days i've seen time come and go like the seasons
of youth and past dreams left to fend for themselves
and i beheld a pipe in a vision that was not mine to share with
strangers that felt the need to learn to touch to experience
the joy that was us as we travelled between the spirit world and
our own where we could feel and breathe like those before us
but we were banished from this land of those that went before
time erased our memories leaving us scattered and scarred
unable to dream in colour or not knowing the rhythm of the
season
why are we here now remembering in bits and pieces
and the night never-ending waking me from nightmares not of
my making
i scrambled from my past
stumbling in place
dancing i tried to leave
but i was held in awe by my ineptness
and you laughed and laughed
my clumsy attempts at trying to find my feet again
long ago i stopped giving thanks
and the dreams that were visions were left discarded behind me
buried with my mother in a residential room
stark naked except for a cross on a wall
making a sign of the cross and a wish
never fulfilled
we stayed behind while we watched you drive away

yesterday's song

i wish i could slip into muskeg and spruce
encircling myself with northern lights
wolf songs and night hawks rustling the underbrush
catching the smells of the past still on me
even though my feet are concrete hardened
and my spirit tells stories of neon and blues
i am the son of muskeg and spruce
i still dance to the music of yesterday

this city is red

Built on the bones of a thousand generations, this city is main street, each generation with its own stories told in back alleys and city core, hells kitchen, little chicago, with cracked blood filled sidewalks tell tales of broken bodies and defeated minds, nightmares released with each bottle emptied, inhaling a bag full of poison with visions, just to live another day, muting out the voices that hold your memories and enemies, this city is red, north end country song red, a promise followed down from a northern road, seeking a dream armed only with hope, walking down portage to wolseley to st. james then north again, with the same answer, no room, no job, don't bother me, I'll call the cops, shoulders lowered we carry on, finding solace in a pipe full of dreams, watching a liquid filled needle enter vein, fill with blood then empty again, spinning, spinning, always out of control, the room goes round and round, it doesn't seem so bad now, there's always tomorrow, a brighter happier day ahead, these are only dreams, we can't fly, this city is red, full of lies, deceit and false promises, full of fumbling bumbling young suburban men in fancy cars with fancy ideas, full of hate and venom, they cruise selkirk, low track, higgins and main in the cover of darkness, they hunt the weak and the poor, who spit out your semen and take your cash, but they leave a little bit of themselves in you, regardless of your misplaced anger, you disgust yourself, they know you'll be back, your hate doesn't disguise your need, this city is red, it can be ugly and beautiful at the same time, pure white snow of winter hides the needles and the pain, sound of the drum, muted by the walls, regalia of colour flash across a gymnasium floor, the song echoes off the walls, slips through the crack of the door, the song echoes off the walls and travels down main and selkirk, west to st. james, bouncing off portage to tuxedo, blinds closed to silence the drum, nothing changes but the year, this city is red, ceremony red, silent witness to the past, held in darkness, rattling the bones that hold memories, rattle and drum speaks the old language, this song is older than this memory, voices whisper through the ghost dancer wrapped in blankets, he breaks free and speaks the old way again, this city is red, I can walk it at night, hidden in shadows, my footsteps echo yours, you walk/run to avoid your fear, that fear is me, daytime finds me invisible, you see what you only want to see, venting your rage in the local rag, haven't we paid enough, what more do they want, get a job, work like everyone else, an eyesore, better dead than red, this city is red, a colour divided only by imaginary borders afraid to cross, hiding our faces into ourselves, but some of us sneak across those invisible lines, we tell stories, we laugh, we cry, we heal, we dance, we sing, our heartbeat is the drum, we wake the bones that rattle your hate, this city is dirty, but it's farmer dirty, blowing in from the prairies, white skin browned by the summer sun, knows this land, they are my neighbours, this city hides its hate but we have felt it for so long, we know it's there, buried beneath the manicured lawns, behind the drapes, inside your gates, the shadows hold your fears, holding onto your lies, this city is red, main street red, white, blue sirens criss-cross its face, the hunter becomes the hunted, covering his tracks and scent with the stink of back alleys, no one ventures there after dark, we speak to ghosts that live there, dumped outside the city limits, we become bones, part of a forgotten story, one line in the pages of this city's past, filed away as a statistic, an unfortunate ending to a heartbeat, this city is red, a blood red history you have chosen to ignore and when you become dust, I will dance on your ashes, when the seed of a new flower blossoms, after your ashes have settled becoming one with the soil, I will dance again

sleeping with eyes wide open
mind wanders in and out
range of voices speaking in tongues
long thought lost buried in stone tablets
confusion within
no comprehension
sleeping with eyes wide open
fade in fade out
becoming blurred in my memory
where that first appeared
listing all my sins for all to see
unable to defend myself I sought penance in dreams
sleeping with eyes wide open
memories scattered
strewn haphazardly
fragments of life left behind
without rhyme or reason
swept beneath a dream
vision interrupted
imagination easily distracted
cobwebbed thoughts dust covered in the attic of my mind
sudden recognition of a familiar scent
between chance meetings on travels behind the Windsor
the music book marking the nights
losing ideas behind a haze of smoke

drifting between worlds
back alley paths littered with spent prophylactics
the soft footsteps and quiet moans
echo, echo, echo, echo
but the words of the song
remain within the walls of red city
and the freaks, gangbangers and wannabes crawl out of the 'burbs
into the neon lit background of a downtown thought abandoned
til you peel back the dirt and concrete
looking to score
and when you rise above the stink and smog
with self induced visions
one can see the distance without borders or horizons
leaving reality unimpeded
we walk the silent streets after the city sleeps
we sing
this city is red
this city is red
i know the trails hidden beneath the concrete paths
i listen carefully
when the moon is full
i still hear its heartbeat
and the chant is never forgotten
the old ones never left
they never stopped dancing
that beat that lies beneath the soil
is slowly waking
red city

(revised September 2019)*

---

* This poem began as a performance piece in the early 2000s, and it changed and expanded over many performances. A youtube video entitled "MIWF 2014 – Duncan Mercredi – 'This City is Red'" documents a performance at the Winnipeg Indigenous Writers' Festival in January 2014. Another version of the poem was also published in *Prairie Fire* magazine in 2017.

Three solitudes

This city
Sings a quiet song
Meeting at the junction of two rivers
Background song of drum and dance
Echoes of laughter and tears
Buried beneath the concrete
Sacred mounds long leveled
Meaning nothing
Needing space to build
Lay tracks
Displayed in glass cases
This city
Dirty sidewalks cover blood and death
A spirit left to lie alone
No name, no reason
Just a body, buried in back pages
A shrug, move on
I have lived here longer than where I was born
I walk along its concrete trails
Paths have led me through back alley dreams
Still my visions take me back
That place where the river blessed me
I could dive down deep within that clear cold water
Stretch my arms out to touch bottom
But I never could and over time
That clear cold water became cloudy
No longer clear
No longer life giving
No longer blessed
Now I haunt the urban landscape
Searching for another song
One I heard as a child
Has faded by city sounds and sirens in the night
Reaching the place where the city ends
All I see is an unending horizon
I always turn back
Face east, west, south but never north
I have left that place
I have placed my tobacco on these sidewalks
To claim this city as my home

I have done my time
Carried my share through summers and winters
I have walked those hidden trails
Followed a scent I once remembered
I have fallen
I have left a blood trail
Not knowing where it began
I have lost weekends and days
My mind cloaked with other world images
Full of color and sound
I have done my time
In the silence footfall of hidden paths
Lost then found again
Skirting a raging river
My furs piled on my back
Weighed down by a birch bark canoe
My song in Cree and French
Drifting from my lips on my sweat that hit the ground
Beneath me
To slip into the dirt
Evaporating with the birth of the new sun
Trying to catch a hand sacrificed to the river
I have done my time
My name was not mine
My words rang hollow
Yours imprinted squaw man you knew me as
While I worked beside you
Never crossing that invisible line that set us apart
Going our own way when day was done
You entered accepted you told me once
I entered ridiculed with a new label
Apple
I have done my time
I was raised to follow my father's and uncles' footsteps
In my dreams and in my visions they are covered with ice
And scars from felling trees and bloodied hands from setting traps
The room with the scent of sweetgrass and pelts
Casting shadows on walls inside the house
Squinting at the book I held in my hands

My kookum's stories melding with the story I read
I have done my time

that river fed us
Quenched our thirst
She was our playground four seasons
She carried our dreams and hopes on her journey to the lake
I floated on her at dusk
Counting stars as the night awakened
while listening to a whippoorwill sing a goodnight song
I have done my time
Watched the silence blasted out of its reverie
The dust blinded us night and day
We were introduced to another reality
We weren't ready
But I found it fascinating
And I swore I would find its source
My footsteps echo down portage and main
agamik to a place where the streets were empty   *across the river*
Even during the day
Words some I understood whispered behind covered windows
A flutter of drapes and an eye peeking out as I walk by
I had entered the second solitude
I have done my time

(2018)

Getting jiggie

Hey, I say
Just jiggie with the folks
Lookin' at me like my mind is gone
Little do they know
Yeah cut the talk
The street too hard to handle
Used to dance there once
Got caught lookin' sideways
Hey, I say
Been lookin' for a ride
Just after midnight
Ground feelin' shaky and headin' my way
Saw you on the avenue
Lookin' kind of lost
Kept turnin' your back to the wind
No hidin' from that in this place
Wind finds you here no matter where you hide
And no matter where you make your bed
Hey, I say
Need to move on
Can't stand out here
Lookin' like I need a kick
Shakin' from the season
Birds headin' south
Me, gotta head north
Place where I make my bed
Later, man
Catch you again next time
Hey, I say
Did I just hear a harp echo in the wind
From across the street
Maybe I'll step inside
Just for one more
One that will carry me home
Hey, I say
later

(2015)

omasinayikesis   *one who keeps records*

I don't know what sacredness is
I cannot sit there in front of you
to say what you can and can not do
I do not know why women cannot enter the circle
Unless they wear a dress or skirt
I can't say why an offering is placed
Or tobacco offered for council or story
I am not versed in protocol
I merely understand what is polite
I never experienced a circle as a child

(2019)

Drowning

Now years later
After the fact
You want to learn who i am
All i can say
You are learning from a man without a past
Parts of which were wiped clean
By the stroke of your pen
Now you say you are sorry
Too late
But what you once thought you were was no longer there
The damage had occurred while I was forced to sleep
Leaving behind all that i was
Drowning under the weight of your laws
Ones you considered unfair
Then fled
But you had wrapped them in a blanket you gave as a gift
You then bestowed upon me a vision of rebirth after death
When I couldn't grasp the concept
You paganized my beliefs

(2018)

Tin can skates

Campbell's soup, Libby's beans cans shaped to fit over moccasins
Uncle George's pond shoveled and swept
Willows cut and shaped to look like sherwoods
The rush to pick the side to defend
Sides not picked
The game was to chase the puck made from spruce saplings
Goal nets were overshoes
Defended by Jack Bernard (he was the youngest and smallest)
Racing across the pond as puck was chased (he guarded both goals)
Tossing his stick at the puck
Yelling, wait, wait, let me get ready
Quickly changing direction as puck changed ends
Tripping sliding tumbling over each other
Jo-Jo, nipi! Elma the door calling, Jo-jo running to the house to get some water
Hurrying back to rejoin the game
Another voice, Ener, nipi, he'd be gone
Tossing his tin can skates aside
Returning, out of breath
"Where's my tin can skates" (Jack Bernard had buried them in the snow)
Grabbing another pair of tin can skates from the pile
Slipping them on, rejoining the game
Forgetting what side he was on
Breakaways thwarted by tossing sticks at tin can skates knocking them off, laughter echoing down kanaschack
Game forgotten for a time while trying to knock tin can skates off others feet
Quick run into auntie Louise's house for a quick sip of hot tea
(she always kept a pot of tea on the stove)
Back to the game
Sides didn't matter
Game was to chase the puck
A shot, puck splinters into a dozen pieces
Looking for another to replace it
(Jack Bernard had buried them, scramble to see where he hid them)
A breakaway, toss the stick, knock the tin can skates off, slip, slide, run into Jack Bernard, the yell, "I'm telling!"
Auntie, mom and kookum look out the window
All three calling, "don't pick on the little man"

Faces wind burned, winter breath drifts away in the breeze
paymeetsu, paymeetsu, echoes from auntie Josephine's and auntie
    charlotte's
George, Pinase, Ener scramble home
paymeetsu, paymeetsu, Jake, Norbert and Leslie toss off their tin can
    skates
paymeetsu, paymeetsu, mom is at the door, Jack Bernard, Jo-jo, Charlie
    and myself
Slowly walk back to the house
(Charlie lived past Campbell's store and would eat lunch with us)
Crumple bannock and homemade bread into the ruffed grouse soup
Steaming hot, sipping it slow, only the murmurs of kookum, Elma and
    mom's voice in the background
We need wood
Dress, go back to pond, gather our tin can skates and pile them
George would be sawing logs at his house
Pinsae would be chopping theirs while Ener would gather the wood and
    load his sled
Jack Bernard would sit on the logs placed on the saw horse to steady them
While Jo-jo and Charlie worked the saw
I'd gather what they cut and pile them
We'd take turns chopping them in half and take them into the porch
Uncle George would be on the pond, picking up the pieces of our
    splintered spruce sapling pucks
Then cleaning the ice
To be ready for another round of tin can skates hockey in misipawistik
    1950's style

(2019)

who will wipe my tears

how will you answer
when your child asks you
what did you do when you watched
us take our last breath
what did you do
when the last river was silenced
and the water no longer gave life
where did you go to count your seven pieces of silver
did you wipe my tears knowing
that I meant so little to you
did you answer
when I asked you why

(2020)

iskotawan   *the fire is still on (burning)*

kookum sits in the shadows now
Watching
Listening
Her stories flow through me
She watches
Silently
kookum sits in the shadows now
Watching
Listening
My stories now
Part of hers
But mine are angrier
She whispers through the ages
kiyam. kiyam   *it doesn't matter*
achimo   *tell a story*
ekosi ta kiskentam   *this way they will know*
nata apo nookum   *over there my kookum sits*
kayask itew   *long time ago she says*
Her voice fades
Mine rises
kookum sits in the shadows now
But we still speak the same language
Our stories change
Yet remain the same
ekosi   *that's all for now*

(2019)

Afterword

I think sometimes what you write is interpreted differently from what you were trying to convey by some people, they see from their eyes, not wanting to see from the writer's point of view, it can be disturbing and goes against everything you were raised to believe, they want to see, but what they were taught does not allow them to explore further what the storyteller is saying, in other words, they don't listen to what you hear.

I've been thinking about a photograph of me when I was based at 8 mile channel in '71–'72. I don't have any pictures of me at the other work camps I stayed in before 8 mile channel. Those camps were in Minago River and Williams Lake, both north of Misipawistik (Grand Rapids) and I was working for the highways department at the time. After the completion of Highway 6 connecting to Highway 391 (now Hwy. 6) and three months off, I was sent to Soab Lake, southwest of Thompson, and when that contract was finished, I was transferred to Thompson. After two months I left and moved back to Winnipeg, thinking my bush camp days were done with and I looked for work closer to home. Nothing materialized, a young Cree/Métis man was way down on the list as a potential employee of most companies in Winnipeg at that time. An old world man, a finishing carpenter, took a chance and hired me, it was mostly part time work but I liked it. Then hydro called and at the time the job looked promising and off to 8 mile channel I went, with two to three months on site and six days off, except at Christmas, that was two weeks off. Come June, I decided that after five years of living out of a trailer and a backpack, it was time to look for something else.

All those years, I only worked with white men with one exception, 8 mile channel, where there was one other Indigenous man from Norway House, he left shortly after Christmas. You spend a lot of time alone in those camps, small as they were, most of the men stayed to themselves, even with two-man rooms, very little was shared in way of conversations, bits and pieces of small talk, nothing personal between you and your roommate. Quiet meals, most conversations were spoken in hushed voices, I learned very quickly to sit by myself, eat fast and leave, either to get to work or back to my room.

Isolation within isolation, you learned to adapt to the silence. I became an observer, always "in the shadows," listening, watching, staying silent unless a comment was made belittling people like me, then I would respond and that is why the cook shack would become silent when I came in to eat. I carried that silence home and it almost ended my relationship.

I always knew who I was, I just didn't know where I belonged. I was a stranger to those I worked with and I became a stranger to those I grew up with. That photograph with that slight smile is the only one I have from that time that actually shows me with that little smile. I think I had already made up my mind then, I was leaving the camp once summer came.

In all that time I worked at these camps and from the time my daughter was born until she was able to talk, I was Duncan to her, this strange quiet man who made her laugh when he would suddenly appear for a few days, then disappear again for months. She was four before she called me "dad."

After five years I didn't want to end up like all those men who only viewed life from what they learned in the bush camps and spoke in whispers, if they spoke at all. I worked night shift most of the time, just me and another man in the wheelhouse of the dredge, 8 hours of silence, 7 days a week, 2 months or more, the only words we spoke were, "see you tonight."

I never said good-bye to anyone when I left the 8 mile camp, except to my roommate, I left without looking back.

I don't know why we searched out the darkness when we first moved to the city. My wife Freida had already been here for two years before me. She was raising our daughter with help from her mother while I worked up north in the bush camps, some with Manitoba hydro, other times it was with the department of highways. My visits were sporadic, never really knowing when the contractor would shut the construction down to allow his crews some downtime, especially the companies that were working on highways. Camps changed as contracts were completed, moving from one site to another, and time off was dictated by where a new camp would be located and then how long it would take to set up. If it was a week, it meant a week off, if it was three days, three days off, not much time to get down to the city when the trip was a six- to eight-hour drive. Working for hydro was different, it was two months in camp then six days off. It was always a scramble to get to Winnipeg, get reacquainted with Freida and my daughter, do some shopping, but always, always the need to see and do everything one could do with the time I had to visit, go to movies, and of course, the strip. It was night after night of bar hopping, not caring, just going.

Back in Misipawistik we used to walk the old portage that the old ones used to skirt the rapids. We didn't know how old the trail was but it was easy to find. It was well-worn, nothing grew on that trail, wide enough to see that one could carry a canoe loaded down with furs and not brush against the trees and bush that grew beside it. We'd run down that path, not loaded down with furs or canoes, just what we needed to spend the day on that trail. We didn't carry any lunches, what we needed, we hunted, fish were easy to catch and there were always grouse, ruff tailed, sharp tail, spruce hens, easily available and so easy to bring down. We went from end to end on that portage, right from across kanaschack (the point) to the head of the rapids.

We got to know that trail like the backs of our hands, a place we explored all summer long and well into the fall. But there was one spot we always stopped at, the highest point of the trail, a site where one could find remains of old campfires, scattered pieces of bones, discarded pails used as cooking pots. We'd stop there to eat, just like others had stopped generations before us.

But that's not the only reason we stopped there, we had another reason. It was a place we tested ourselves, our resolve, our fear. It was the place where the rapids curved from east-southeast to northwesterly and a place where the rapids were the swiftest and the loudest, a place where we had to shout to talk to each other, a place we both feared and that gave us exhilaration, a place where we knew the old ones watched as we played our most dangerous game.

About ten paces from where we ate was the edge of the bank, from the edge was a trail that wound its way down the bank, about 150 feet down to the edge of the water, at that place was a small area where the rapids didn't reach, about ten feet of calmness, and at the very end of the trail was a little spruce tree, bent, remains of branches still visible on one side. We would all stand next to that trail, looking down, then our oldest cousin would take off down that trail, running straight down, slipping and sliding, never slowing down and at the very last moment, just before slipping into the water, he would grab at the spruce tree to stop himself, watching it bend, but never breaking. Holding him there at the edge. We all took turns, from oldest to youngest, eyes glued to the edge as it rushed towards you, everything beside you a blur, eyes focused on that small tree, slipping, sliding, trying to maintain balance as you hurtled down that trail, then reaching, reaching for that small tree, fingers just brushing those last remains of a branch, feeling the coldness of the water, that cold dark rushing water filling your shoes, unable to hang on, and a hand reaching out, grabbing your shirt, pulling you back, just before the rapids took hold of you. Hearing the laughter, and a voice, kaygatch (that was close), climbing back up the trail to continue on our way. Then taking off my pants but keeping the shoes on.

On the way back, we'd play the game again.

Memories

Memories of others long since passed, appear from time to time, depending on the song and the season

    The chill of an early winter as evening falls brings you to mind

    And our breaths would mingle beneath the evening star while a solitary note from a solitary harp would echo across the sky

    And the song would disappear into the cedar and spruce while the softness of the muskeg would cushion our passion and muffle our sighs of want and need but the song would end before we crossed that threshold until the echo of another song would reverberate through the night dancing with the northern lights and once again our passion would rise and fall with each string strummed

    Caressing and coaxing a reluctant voice to sing a song of joy in the key of blue

Bar smelling of after midnight

Voice of the street drifting in and out with each opening and closing of the door a cue ball a silent nod corner pocket by the back door smelling of after midnight and the blues man the blues always on the street rumbling dancing to the music of low riders hogs filling the bar with wind-burned faces and hair combed by the wind, bar smelling of after midnight full of bikers, smokers, night off hookers, wannabees, can't bes, VLTers, across the street drop ins, cross dressers and suburbanites, old friends, new friends all smiling that good to see you smile but the blues man the blues all nod fridays smelling of after midnight at the corner of St. Mary and Garry.

Chameleon

A blue collar guy in a white collar world living in a tie-dyed neighborhood writing in broken english dreaming in cree in a concrete forest my skin a chameleon of colors from a whiter shade of red in spring to the dark brown of summer to the earth tones of fall and then the darker shade of white in winter and you ask me why are you confused

    I had another reason I walked as far as the forks this morning, I was seeking an answer from the old ones, I know, I know, I'm not the most spiritual or traditional person and I am a skeptic on our beliefs, but there are times I have to toss out all those "I don't believe it" ideas, today was one of those days, I want to tell you about my mother, now I am more like my mother than my father, although I've been told I look more like the Mercredi side of the family rather than the Thomas side, but I watched my mother a lot when I was a child, the way she talked, her silent moments, the way she would drift away, even in a room full of people, she always said to me, on those late nights after too many drinks, "I have no place I can call home, I live here (meaning Grand Rapids), I was born there, (meaning Nelson House) but these places are not 'home,' I don't know what a home feels like." My mother, auntie and uncle left Nelson House to go to residential school (Brandon), she was 8, auntie was 5, uncle was 9, uncle stayed less than 2 years, he contracted tb when he was there, our grandfather went and got him, not wanting him to die in a strange place but also determined to cure him, he did, took him home to his trapline and fought that disease that took so many, he won and he never sent uncle back to that school, my mother and auntie stayed, for years before coming home for the summer, mother told me once, made me swear to never tell this to anyone, but she's gone now, so I can, she said, "when I got to our house, my mom was hanging sheets on the clothesline, when I saw her I was so angry at her I couldn't hug her, all those years she never came down to visit, never once, it took me years to understand why she didn't."

    I used to walk with my mother to go visit the Garricks, they lived across the bay from kanaschack, we'd have to cross a few creeks to get to their house, this old house, hidden by trees and willows, it looked enormous to me, I'd sit and stare at their china cabinet, filled with her cups and plates and other treasures, I was allowed to look at them but not touch, I'd sit there and listen to them talk, never taking my eyes from that display, she loved visiting the Garricks, the walk home would be silent, but then all our walks would be, we'd stop at kanaschak and pick what fruit was in season.

Afterword / 73

My mother was happiest when she was singing or dancing, she lived for the dances in the village, then later after the dance, when she thought everyone was asleep, she'd sit at the table, drinking tea, I'd sneak down the stairs, stay in the shadows, watch her, this lonely woman who believed she had no place to call home, watch her as she wiped the tears from her eyes. That's why I walked to the forks, to ask the old ones if I could share this little story of my mother, they didn't say no and they didn't say yes.

I was going to wear orange, then I thought I don't need orange to remind me or to never forget, one doesn't forget when one lived with those memories, from somewhere deep down inside those memory banks they would emerge, it took a lot of drinks to drag those nightmares to the surface, one doesn't forget that heartache told to you late at night, long after last call, quietly, not to wake the young ones. Now, the settlers, they should wear orange, to remind them, it happened, it didn't go away, it's not something "to let go, it's in the past," the old ones they know, until all their stories are told, they will never let us forget.

I love my walks, that breeze carries many stories.

Heading north again tomorrow, time of departure, unknown, time of arrival, before dark, traveling companion, undecided, reason, visit old sites, reconnect, what once lived there, like this one, "we lived here, Kookum's house, Uncle George close by, we could see Uncle Isadore's place just past the graveyard, from our yard, we shared what we planted in Kookum's garden, next to the river was Yourba's little house, next to church," now I walk on it, nothing is the same, their history bulldozed over, they did not erase my memories, that D9 did not touch those.

Something to share

Kind words were spoken, funny memories were shared, others stayed silent, tears were shed, others, I'm sure, wondered why, family crowded a small space to pay their respects, food was gifted to those who came and laughter was given in return, as for me, there was a sadness, not that she left when she did, because for me, she left years ago, visiting her, I was a stranger, I'd watch her, quietly, while she searched her memory, trying to put a name to that face that said, "hi Clara, it's me," but rarely would recognition register in her eyes, occasionally a little bit of light would appear, not often though, and I would wonder if it was the voice she connected with or maybe the scent he or she carried, and my mind would wander back as Freida would sit beside her, sometimes holding her hand, adjusting her blanket on her shoulders, trying to make this body as comfortable as she could, my thoughts drifting back to when my mother was younger, those nights she'd come home after a dance from someone's house, she'd sit with my father, sharing a cup of tea, whispering, he'd go to bed, she would stay up a bit longer, washing the few dishes that had been left out, I always stayed up until she would join my father in their bed, hiding in the shadows of the stairs, she always looked lonely at those times, I remember those nights, watching her dance, laughing and chatting with everyone, then that loneliness that seemed to descend on her when the house got quiet as it drifted off into sleep, I always wondered why, then there were those other times, upstairs, where we kept the old turntable, remember those, the old crank them up turntables, played the old 78s, the faster you cranked the faster they played, those ones, we'd be up there, upstairs, brother Jack, little sister Adele, father would ask us to put a record on, their favorite, "mom and dad waltz," Lefty Frizzell, and they'd waltz, father and mother, not once but over and over until brother Jack would get tired of it and crank that handle to speed up that old 78 until they would stop, laughing as they did, real laughter, from the heart, another memory, watching her iron the clothes she had brought back after burying her daughter, not at home but to her, far from home, that iron, sliding back and forth, back and forth, her tears, drifting down, the quiet ssss as the iron slid over that spot where her tears fell, those memories of her come and go.

    I think we look for ways to destroy ourselves, and if we can't do it to ourselves, we find someone we know who will gladly do it, for one reason, they believe we behave in such a way that you are better than they are, we are our own worst enemies.

—Duncan Mercredi

Acknowledgements

Thanks should go to Neil Besner and Warren Cariou, Neil for asking me if I was interested in having this done and Warren for agreeing to be part of it, but we mustn't forget Melanie Braith for transcribing my choices for this collection, she saved the day, what took her a few hours all the while knitting something, would have taken me days, can't thank them enough. To tell you the truth I didn't think anyone would be interested in my weird way of looking at life and land, and my stubborn stand on having someone edit what I've written, "my words, my mind, my heart, if you want changes, speak to the old ones, they gave them to me," Warren understood that and I'm really thankful for it, I'm sure he shook his head a few times.

lps Books in the Laurier Poetry Series
Published by Wilfrid Laurier University Press

Nelson Ball	*Certain Details: The Poetry of Nelson Ball*, selected with an introduction by Stuart Ross, with an afterword by Nelson Ball • 2016 • xxiv + 86 pp. • ISBN 978-1-77112-246-7
derek beaulieu	*Please, No More Poetry: The Poetry of derek beaulieu*, edited by Kit Dobson, with an afterword by Lori Emerson • 2013 • xvi + 74 pp. • ISBN 978-1-55458-829-9
Dionne Brand	*Fierce Departures: The Poetry of Dionne Brand*, edited by Leslie C. Sanders, with an afterword by Dionne Brand • 2009 • xvi + 44 pp. • ISBN 978-1-55458-038-5
Di Brandt	*Speaking of Power: The Poetry of Di Brandt*, edited by Tanis MacDonald, with an afterword by Di Brandt • 2006 • xvi + 56 pp. • ISBN 978-0-88920-506-2
Nicole Brossard	*Mobility of Light: The Poetry of Nicole Brossard*, edited by Louise H. Forsyth, with an afterword by Nicole Brossard • 2009 • xxvi + 118 pp. • ISBN 978-1-55458-047-7
Alice Burdick	*Deportment: The Poetry of Alice Burdick*, edited by Alessandro Porco • 2018 • xxx + 64 pp. • ISBN 978-1-77112-380-8
Margaret Christakos	*Space Between Her Lips: The Poetry of Margaret Christakos*, edited by Gregory Betts, with an afterword by Margaret Christakos • 2017 • xxviii + 68 pp. • ISBN 978-1-77112-297-9
George Elliott Clarke	*Blues and Bliss: The Poetry of George Elliott Clarke*, edited by Jon Paul Fiorentino, with an afterword by George Elliott Clarke • 2008 • xviii + 72 pp. • ISBN 978-1-55458-060-6
Dennis Cooley	*By Word of Mouth: The Poetry of Dennis Cooley*, edited by Nicole Markotić, with an afterword by Dennis Cooley • 2007 • xxii + 62 pp. • ISBN 978-1-55458-007-1
Lorna Crozier	*Before the First Word: The Poetry of Lorna Crozier*, edited by Catherine Hunter, with an afterword by Lorna Crozier • 2005 • xviii + 62 pp. • ISBN 978-0-88920-489-8
Christopher Dewdney	*Children of the Outer Dark: The Poetry of Christopher Dewdney*, edited by Karl E. Jirgens, with an afterword by Christopher Dewdney • 2007 • xviii + 60 pp. • ISBN 978-0-88920-515-4
Don Domanski	*Earthly Pages: The Poetry of Don Domanski*, edited by Brian Bartlett, with an afterword by Don Domanski • 2007 • xvi + 62 pp. • ISBN 978-1-55458-008-8

Louis Dudek	*All These Roads: The Poetry of Louis Dudek*, edited by Karis Shearer, with an afterword by Frank Davey • 2008 • xx+ 70 pp. • ISBN 978-1-55458-039-2
Paul Dutton	*Sonosyntactics: Selected and New Poetry by Paul Dutton*, edited by Gary Barwin, with an afterword by Paul Dutton • 2015 • ISBN 978-1-77112-132-3
George Fetherling	*Plans Deranged by Time: The Poetry of George Fetherling*, edited by A.F. Moritz, with an afterword by George Fetherling • 2012 • xviii + 64 pp. • ISBN 978-1-55458-631-8
Phil Hall	*Guthrie Clothing: The Poetry of Phil Hall, a Selected Collage* edited by rob mclennan, with an afterword by Phil Hall • 2015 • xvi + 72 pp. • ISBN 978-1-77112-191-0
Robert Kroetsch	*Post-glacial: The Poetry of Robert Kroetsch*, selected with an introduction by David Eso and an afterword by Aritha van Herk • 2019 • xviii + 94 pp. • ISBN 978-1-77112-426-3
M. Travis Lane	*The Crisp Day Closing on My Hand: The Poetry of M.Travis Lane*, edited by Jeanette Lynes, with an afterword by M. Travis Lane • 2007 • xvi + 86 pp. • ISBN 978-1-55458-025-5
Tim Lilburn	*Desire Never Leaves: The Poetry of Tim Lilburn*, edited by Alison Calder, with an afterword by Tim Lilburn • 2007 • xiv + 50 pp. • ISBN 978-0-88920-514-7
Eli Mandel	*From Room to Room: The Poetry of Eli Mandel*, edited by Peter Webb, with an afterword by Andrew Stubbs • 2011 • xviii + 66 pp. • ISBN 978-1-55458-255-6
Daphne Marlatt	*Rivering: The Poetry of Daphne Marlatt*, edited by Susan Knutson, with an afterword by Daphne Marlatt • 2014 • xxiv + 72 pp. • ISBN 978-1-77112-038-8
Steve McCaffery	*Verse and Worse: Selected and New Poems of Steve McCaffery 1989–2009*, edited by Darren Wershler, with an afterword by Steve McCaffery • 2010 • xiv + 76 pp. • ISBN 978-1-55458-188-7
Don McKay	*Field Marks: The Poetry of Don McKay*, edited by Méira Cook, with an afterword by Don McKay • 2006 • xxvi + 60 pp. • ISBN 978-0-88920-494-2
Duncan Mercredi	*mahikan ka onot: The Poetry of Duncan Mercredi*, edited by Warren Cariou, with an afterword by Duncan Mercredi • 2020 • xx + 82 pp. • ISBN 978-1-77112-474-4
Al Purdy	*The More Easily Kept Illusions: The Poetry of Al Purdy*, edited by Robert Budde, with an afterword by Russell Brown • 2006 • xvi + 80 pp. • ISBN 978-0-88920-490-4

Sina Queyras	*Barking & Biting: The Poetry of Sina Queyras*, selected with an introduction by Erin Wunker, with an afterword by Sina Queyras • 2016 • xviii + 70 pp. • ISBN 978-1-77112-216-0
F.R. Scott	*Leaving the Shade of the Middle Ground: The Poetry of F.R. Scott*, edited by Laura Moss, with an afterword by George Elliott Clarke • 2011 • xxiv + 72 pp. • ISBN 978-1-55458-367-6
Sky Dancer Louise Bernice Halfe	*Sôhkêyihta: The Poetry of Sky Dancer Louise Bernice Halfe*, edited by David Gaertner, with an afterword by Sky Dancer Louise Bernice Halfe • 2018 • xx + 96 pp. • ISBN 978-1-77112-349-5
Fred Wah	*The False Laws of Narrative: The Poetry of Fred Wah*, edited by Louis Cabri, with an afterword by Fred Wah • 2009 • xxiv + 78 pp. • ISBN 978-1-55458-046-0
Tom Wayman	*The Order in Which We Do Things: The Poetry of Tom Wayman*, edited by Owen Percy, with an afterword by Tom Wayman • 2014 • xx + 92 pp. • ISBN 978-1-55458-995-1
Rachel Zolf	*Social Poesis: The Poetry of Rachel Zolf*, selected with an introduction by Heather Milne and an afterword by Rachel Zolf • 2019 • xviii + 80 pp. • ISBN 978-1-77112-411-9
Jan Zwicky	*Chamber Music: The Poetry of Jan Zwicky*, edited by Darren Bifford and Warren Heiti, with a conversation with Jan Zwicky • 2014 • xx + 82 pp. • ISBN 978-1-77112-091-3